To an Ancient People

To an Ancient People

JJJ

The Autobiography of Dr. Leopold Cohn

CHOSEN PEOPLE MINISTRIES
New York, New York

IN THE U.S.:

    CHOSEN PEOPLE MINISTRIES
    241 East 51st Street
    New York, NY 10022
    212/223-2252

IN CANADA:

    CHOSEN PEOPLE MINISTRIES (Canada)
    P.O. Box 897 Sta. B
    North York, ON M2K 2R1
    CANADA 416/250-0177

IN ISRAEL:

    Beit Sar Shalom
    P.O. Box 637
    Kfar Saba, Israel
    972-9-958-256

INTRODUCTION

by Leopold Cohn

I have written the following pages in response to the need, expressed by my friends, of a booklet that could be used in presenting to others, in concise and definite form, the importance of giving the Gospel to the Jews. The progress of this Gospel work among the 400,000* Jews of Brooklyn, in which we have labored for over fourteen years, has been so remarkable, and its financial resources so feeble, that they have given themselves to the task of making as many new friends as possible for the work.

Now since the Lord has taken from me that great treasure, my dear wife, whose life was a bright shining light for Messiah, the requests to write of the work, and of the way the Lord Jesus led us to Himself, have increased. Therefore, I decided, after a long and prayerful consideration, to devote my time and energy to the task

---

*Increased to over 1,000,000 before Dr. Cohn's death in 1937, and to 1,937,000 in greater New York in 1994.

of committing this narrative of God's wonderful leadings to print, knowing that in no other way could I so fitly rear a monument to the memory of the dear one that has slipped away from us so early in life than to dedicate this booklet to her. Her heart was so much in the work that I know her soul will be perfectly satisfied if this booklet shall be the means, under God, of stirring up Christian hearts to the work of reaching the Jews.

The reader will, I am sure, overlook the personal allusions; they cannot be avoided in a narrative of this kind....

That this booklet may find its way over land and sea, from mountain to plain, into the hearts of children of God; breaking down barriers of prejudice, enlightening where there is ignorance, winning over where there is indifference, stirring up where there is lethargy, pacifying where there is antagonism — for the spiritual welfare of poor, scattered Israel, and for the glory and honor of the Lord Jesus the Messiah, King of the Jews, is the earnest prayer of

Yours sincerely in His service,

Leopold Cohn
July, 1908
Brooklyn, N.Y.

To an
Ancient People

Early Life and Training

$\mathcal{I}$ was born in 1862 at Berezna, a little town in the east of Hungary, where I was brought up in orthodox Judaism. The Jews there look upon Christianity as a phase of heathenism, for the Catholics openly exhibit their idolatrous habits, prostrating themselves on the public highways before crosses and images, practices greatly abhorred by the Jews because they were forbidden to Israel by Moses. Their priests are generally addicted to drink and are bitter enemies of the Jews, inciting the peasants to injure them in every possible way. Because of these things, I was taught to avoid Gentiles, not even to take a drink of water from their vessels. The Jews know nothing of Jesus Christ and His claims to the Messiahship. They do not connect the two names, but think of Christ simply as referring to the word "cross." They do not know of His teachings or of the existence of a book called the New Testament.

At the age of seven, my father and mother died in the same year and left me to shift for myself as best I could. Thus I early learned to trust God and often prayed Him to teach me His ways. When thirteen years old, I decided to study to be a rabbi or a leader of my people, the most honorable and meritorious life-office for a Jew.

DESCRIPTION OF THE TALMUD

The main study of one who proposes to become a rabbi, is the Talmud. While mentioning this book, may I tell you what it is, as I meet so many Christians who ask, "What kind of a book is the Talmud?"

The Talmud comprises sixty books which contain all the Jewish civil canonical laws. The number of these laws is legion. One commandment of the Decalogue, "Six days shalt thou labour," etc., "but the seventh day is the Sabbath of the LORD thy God," is explained by the Talmudic doctors in four hundred and sixteen sections, each section containing from eight to twenty divisions, giving the most minute directions for the observance of the Talmudic Sabbath laws. The Jews believe that all these, as well as the many thousands of rules and precepts appointed by the wise men are as holy and binding as the ten commandments because they have a tradition that the Pentateuch, which Israel was commanded to put in writing, is only the text, and the Talmud is the explanation God gave to Moses by word of mouth on Mount Sinai. Moses, when he gave written law, delivered also this oral law to the people, who repeated it until fixed in their memory.

Each generation transmitted it to the next, until about the fourth century, A.D. when the different laws and discourses were collected, compiled, written down, and completed. Ever since that time the Jews make these books their chief study, day and night, not only for the sake of knowing the different laws, or of becoming rabbis, but because they believe that in studying the Talmud they render the greatest service to God, as the Talmud itself says, "there is no more meritorious study than that of the oral law." So I was a very good boy when I devoted nearly all my time to the Talmud and almost none to the Prophets.

GRADUATION AND MARRIAGE

At about eighteen years of age I was proficient in Hebrew literature and Talmudic law. I then received from several rabbis, in whose colleges I had studied, a diploma containing a certificate of my good character and a cquirements and also authority to become a rabbi. This was confirmed by my first and chief rabbi, a miracle-performer, S.L. Teitelbaum, in Sziget. In a town nearby lived a wealthy Jew who consulted with this great miracle-performing rabbi about taking me for his son-in-law, as he desired to marry his youngest daughter Rose to a rabbi. When consent was given, I was called, and according to the custom there, arrangement was made as to how large a sum of money the father-in-law was to give me before I married his pretty and highly accomplished young daughter.

Our marriage was consummated in 1880. In the

house of my father-in-law I was very happy, and always thanked God for giving me at last, after much hard labor in studying, so delightful a home. Many marks of honor were shown me, and I received tokens of love and of kindness on all sides and the days I spent under my father-in-law's roof were the brightest in my life. About a year after my marriage, my father-in-law died.

Very soon after my marriage some people began to ask me questions as a rabbi, for they knew that I had attained to that position, but I refused to deal with them, as I lived near to my teacher in Sziget, and it is not lawful for a disciple to decide religious questions while his rabbi lives in the same district. Several years later, when that rabbi died, I was called to practice my rabbinical duties in three congregations. For years they sought the law at my mouth. I decided among them all the different religious questions concerning worship, meat and milk, wine of libation, and the laws concerning slaughtering of animals. If two had a quarrel, which led them to go to the law, they came to me and accepted my decision without further appeal, for such is the Jewish rule. So I was both the lawyer and the judge. Every controversy was settled by my word, and at times I was called to distant places to decide cases, as my methods seemed to be liked.

During my leisure, I had frequent recourse to my Talmud, in which I at one time read the following: "The world is to stand six thousand years, vis., two thousand confusion and void, two thousand with the law, and two thousand the time of Messiah." Rashi, the very first and most authoritative commentator gives as an explanation on the last clause: "Because after the second two thousand years, the Messiah must have come and the wicked kingdom should have been destroyed." This greatly excited my attention. I was accustomed to sit on the ground almost every Thursday night at twelve o'clock, weeping, crying, and mourning for about an hour, over the destruction of Jerusalem (called by the Jews "Tickin Chazoss") and repeating the 137th Psalm.

I was very anxiously awaiting the coming of our Messiah, and now I saw that his time was over two thousand years ago, according to the Jewish reckoning. I was surprised, and asked myself, "Is it possible that the time which God had fixed for the appearance of our Messiah has passed away without the promise of our true and living God being fulfilled?" I never had had any doubt of the truthfulness of the Talmud; I believed every part of it to be holy, but now I looked upon this passage as a simple legend. It was then that I decided to search the Prophets concerning the time of the Messiah.

EARLY RESEARCHES

My first thought was to study Daniel, but I soon recollected that the Talmud curses one who studies concerning the end of the age, especially that part of Daniel which refers to the coming of the Messiah and the end of the times. "The bones of him who studies and calculates the ends" (meaning the time of the Messiah) "shall be blown up," says the Talmud.

This sent terror into my heart and I thought that the minute I began to read that part of Daniel, a thunderbolt would come down from Heaven and strike me dead.

DEFYING THE CURSE

But another thought came, suggesting that those Talmudists who made such statements must themselves have studied Daniel and the other Scriptures, concerning the coming of the Messiah, and if they did it, so would I. With fear and trembling, I opened the book, glanced over it, dwelling particularly on the ninth chapter. My research led me to blame myself for suspecting the holy words of the wise men. While I could see only as through a glass, for I was totally ignorant of Jesus the Messiah, who was cut off not for Himself, and therefore could not understand thoroughly that the Messiah must have died for our sins, yet I realized dimly that the Messiah must have come about four hundred years after Daniel was told by the angel about the seventy weeks.

There was gladness in my heart, to find it true that the Messiah should have come about that time, according to Daniel 9:24. But it was a joy mingled with sorrow. "Why has He not come?" Mind you, dear reader, how you could have gladdened my sorrowful heart by giving me a New Testament, a book whose existence was utterly unknown to me at that time. I, therefore, continued to study the Prophets with greater zeal. Whilst doing so, the pure spirit of God's Word took hold of my mind and heart. I then discovered that much of the Talmudic law is contrary to the Word of God. Then what a great struggle within, between light and darkness! I used to go into my large garden, and under and apple tree, cry like a little child, entreating, "Open thou mine eyes, that I may behold wondrous things out of thy law."

A MEMORABLE FEAST

I could find no rest or peace for my troubled soul. I asked a good many other rabbis about the Messiah and how they reconciled certain passages of the Talmud with the Word of God, but I received no satisfactory answer. A little later, I was preaching, at that season, on a subject connected with the "Feast of Dedication." I had not intended to tell anything publicly of what was so deep in my heart, because of fear of persecution, but God, who causes the dumb to speak, opened my mouth, and I revealed unto them all my discoveries. Probably they would have believed the discovery about the Messiah, since we were all ignorant of the fact that such a disclosure related to the Crucified One, but when they heard me finding so much fault with the holy Talmud, that was quite enough to make them hiss and wag their heads at me, and finally to leave me quite alone, preaching to the empty benches.

Bitter persecution followed.

START FOR AMERICA

I went to a distant town and consulted a noted rabbi, who looked at me in surprise and seemed to grasp the situation. I think he knew something about the Lord Jesus and His claims and did not want to discuss the matter, saying that if he thought and talked about the subject of the Messiah he would be discharged from his position. "But," said he, "my advice is that you go to America. There you will meet plenty of people who will tell you more about the Messiah." So intent was I upon relieving my mind of this burden that I at once set sail for America, determined to find the Messiah at any cost. I did not even return to my home to inform my family that I was going.

About the middle of March, 1892, I found myself in the great city of New York. My countrymen, many of whom knew me personally at home, others by name only, gave me the kindest reception, some even leaving their business to welcome me, when they heard of my arrival. I soon went to a rabbi of my own countrymen, to whom I had a letter of recommendation. He received me very kindly, offering me temporary service in his synagogue and promising to procure a congregation where I could be the rabbi. It was a busy time with the Jews, the time of preparation for the Feast of Unleavened Bread, or the Passover.

DISCOVERIES IN NEW YORK

On the third Saturday after my arrival, I went out for a walk, musing and thinking again about the Messiah, and passed by a church where there was a sign with Hebrew letters saying, "Meetings for Jews." I stopped, became curious and desired to enter. At my first step toward the door, however, I saw a cross at the top of the building. I was puzzled, and began to reason thus, "If this is a Christian Church, what does that Hebrew writing mean? And what connection have they with the Jews? How can a Jew enter a building on which there is a 'cross,' that object which the so-called Christians in my country worship? And how are the Jew and Christian, between whom there is such great hatred in my country, here united?"

As I stood musing and absorbed in these thoughts one of my friends passed by and said, in an awe-inspiring tone: "Mr. Cohn, you had better come away from there." "Why?" asked I. "Just come, please," said he, and was so persistent that I had to follow. We went a few steps when he said, "There are some apostates in that church who mislead our Jewish brethren." "How, how I pray?" for he made me only more anxious to know. He told me at last. "They say that the Messiah has already come." When I heard that, I was nearly bewildered with joy and surprise, for this confirmed my discovery. I longed to enter that church to hear their ideas, but how could I get rid of my companion? I had already taken a lesson in my country not to speak about such things, so I freed myself from him by saying, "Good-bye, friend, I have to go somewhere."

Glancing back until convinced of his disappearance, I ran hastily into the church, notwithstanding the cross at the top. But alas! What a scene! The preacher on the platform, as well as the audience, all bareheaded! What a sin, especially for a rabbi to be bareheaded. I turned quickly and went out, but the janitor, noticing all this, after an interview, gave me the address of the preacher.

MY FIRST NEW TESTAMENT

The following Monday, I called on the minister and found him a Hebrew-Christian with a most interesting, winning way. He was educated in Talmudic literature and when he told me that he was a descendant of a certain well-known rabbi, he gained my confidence and love at once. Seeing my utter ignorance of the Christian faith, but also my great earnestness, he gave me a Hebrew New Testament, asking me to read it. I opened it at once and read for the first time in my life: "This is a book of the generation of Yeshua, the Messiah, the Son of David, the Son of Abraham."

My feelings could not be described! For many years my thoughts had been occupied almost continually with the coming of the Messiah. For that reason I had suffered and left my wife and children for a strange country, which I never expected to visit. I had inquired of several rabbis, searched the Scriptures, prayed and thought; my whole being was wrapped up in this one subject. And now at last here was a book that would tell me about the Messiah. "Surely," I thought, "this book has come to me directly from above. God has sent it to me, and it will give all the desired information and lead me to the Messiah." The words, "Yeshua, the Messiah, the Son of David, the Son of Abraham" were sweeter to me than angelic music.

I forgot all about my troubles and became very happy, and running as fast as I could to my private room, the doors of which I locked behind me, sat down to study that book. I began reading at eleven o'clock in the morning, and continued until one o'clock after midnight. I could not understand the contents of the whole book, but I could at least realize that the Messiah's name was Yeshua, that He was born in Bethlehem, that He had lived in Jerusalem and talked to my people, and that He came just about the time indicated by the angel's message to Daniel. My joy was unbounded.

TRIALS BEGIN

In the morning, I ran quickly to my rabbi friend, who by that time had already a prospect of securing a rabbinical charge for me, and told him of the book and my discoveries. I had not identified this Yeshua, the Messiah, with the name Jesus; I did not see at that time that this Messiah is the same of whom gross caricatures had been presented in my country, neither could I think of Gentiles believing in the Jewish Messiah. Had that been the case, humanly speaking, I could not have been reconciled to that hated Crucified One. I thought that this Yeshua, the Messiah, must be somewhere in this country, ruling as the King, having His people, perhaps the lost ten tribes, as His subjects, and what happiness it would be for me to join them and to be under His rule! Such impossible dreams were in my heart, and when I suggested them to the rabbi, one can imagine what followed.

Vehemently and with terrible curses, he threw the book to the floor, stomped upon it, and in very unkind expressions, denounced me and said that that was the book which the Crucified One had made and it was the cause of all Jewish troubles. "And now," he said, "a Jew like you should not handle that book, or talk, or think of it."

I fled from his wrath with new struggles in my heart. "Is it possible that Yeshua, the Messiah, the Son of David, is the very same person whom the Christians worship? Why, that is idolatry! How can I have anything to do with that?" For several days my heart ached with sorrow and depression. Then I renewed my studies and began to see the truth more plainly, as the sufferings of the Messiah were revealed to me.

The fifty-third chapter of Isaiah was a most wonderful revelation, but what of it? How could I love that hated One? How could I take His name upon my lips since He is the Crucified One and since His followers in every generation and in every country have hated my people, robbed my brothers of all that was good and fair, killed, tortured and degraded them? How could I, a true Jew, join myself to such a band of the enemies of my own flesh and blood? But a small voice seemed to whisper in my heart, "If He is the One of whom the Scriptures write, then you must love Him. No matter what others do in His name, you must do as He teaches."

THE LIGHT DAWNS

Halting between two opinions, I decided to fast a day and pray to God to show me what to do. At noon time, when instead of eating I began to pray, I held in my hands the Hebrew Old Testament and as I cried to God my body shook and the book dropped to the floor and opened for itself. Opening my eyes, I looked down and to my great consternation, read from the open page in the Hebrew, Malachi 3:1, which says literally, "I am sending my messenger and he shall prepare the way before me and the Lord whom you seek shall suddenly come to His temple, even the angel of the covenant" (that word is identical with the word "testament") "whom ye delight in: behold, He has already come, says the Lord of Hosts"!

I fairly began to shiver; like an electric shock the words went through my whole system, and I felt as if the Crucified One stood beside me, pointing to that verse and particularly to the expression, "Behold, He has come already." I was awestricken and fell upon my face exclaiming with all my heart, "My Lord, my Messiah, Yeshua, thou art the One in whom Israel is to be glorified. Thou art surely the One who has reconciled Thy people unto God. From this day, I will serve Thee." At that moment, a flood of light came into my mind and a stream of love to the Lord Jesus into my heart, and straightway I went and took a meal, breaking my fast and feeling altogether a new creature.

RESULTS OF CONFESSION

Then I began with gladness to tell any Jews I met that I had found out that Jesus, the Crucified One, was our Messiah, and not until we as a people accepted Him, would we ever gain favor in the sight of God. At first they thought that I was joking; then they said that I felt lonesome for having left my wife and children whom I loved so dearly, in the old country; my mind was affected and I was not responsible for my words. But as I persevered, they began to be more attentive to my condition and realizing that I was just as sane as ever, they persecuted me bitterly.

They said: "He is a traitor; he has forsaken our religion, our people and our God, and it would be a service to God if some one would lay hands upon him and kill him." (The Jews are no murderers, but their ignorant zeal for God knows no bounds.) They wrote the news to my wife in Europe and someone called a rabbi friend in the old country that I had become an apostate, which means a bad Gentile, whose business is to hate, rob and kill the Jews.

It was a terrible shock to my friends in Hungary, and especially to my dear wife and immediate relatives. The Jews having a real zeal for God, but not according to knowledge, tried to do everything in their power to bring about an absolute separation between me and my wife and children so that they too should not become apostates like me. All communications between my wife and myself were stopped.

A GREAT STRUGGLE

In the meantime, the persecution in New York was so great that I had to flee to Scotland; a German pastor from New York accompanied me to Edinburgh, and introduced me to Rev. Dr. Wilson, pastor of the Barclay Church, and remained there to see me baptized. After having been questioned by the pastor and the elders of the church at a Wednesday evening prayer-meeting, it was agreed that I should be baptized the following Sunday morning, June 26, 1892. That memorable morning impressed itself upon my heart with an indelible power. It was to me like Wellington's Waterloo. I had many enemies in New York, from whose persecution I had to flee, but that day, I met only one foe who would have been almost unconquerable, had it not been for the prayers of God's children.

Early that morning, about daybreak, I awakened with a shiver, and it seemed as if someone spoke saying, "What are you going to do today?" I sprang out of bed and walked up and down the room like one suffering from high fever, almost not knowing what I was doing. I had previously been anxiously waiting to be baptized as I was looking forward with joy to the time when I could publicly confess the Lord Jesus before men, but now a sudden change came over me.

The voice that seemed talking to me was that of the great enemy of mankind, though, of course, he was so sly that I could not at that time know that it was Satan. Very many questions were proposed to me rapidly one after another, and perplexed me so that I felt ill, mentally and physically. He questioned thus: "You are going to be baptized, aren't you? Do you know that as soon as you take this step, you are cut off from your wife whom you love so dearly? She can never live with you again. Do you realize that your four children, of whom you are so fond, will never call you 'papa' or look into your face again? Your brothers, your sisters, all your relatives will consider you dead and their hearts will be broken forever. How can you be so cruel to your own flesh and blood? Your own people will despise and hate you more than ever before. You are a stranger here; you are cutting yourself off from your people; you have no friends in this world. You will be left alone to drift like a piece of timber on the ocean. What will become of you? You will lose your name, your reputation, your official position."

These thoughts put to me in the form of almost audible questions by Satan, whom I for the first time met as a personal enemy, distressed and almost unbalanced my mind. I could not sleep, neither could I eat. My friend who was with me, noticing this, tried to strengthen and encourage me in every way possible, but nothing availed. I knelt down in prayer to God, but that Satanic delusion was as strong as before.

BAPTISM IN EDINBURGH

The time came to go to church. My pastor friend from America went with me and endeavored to cheer me, but awful sorrow and heaviness were in my heart. I merely went to church for the sake of my friend, for I was almost determined to refuse to be baptized that morning, and put it off for another time. The service began and the call came for me to go up to the platform.

No one can imagine the terrible state of my mind, neither could I describe it. Walking up the aisle, I determined to say that I felt too ill for the baptismal rite and ask that it be postponed until next Sunday, but as I reached the platform, a sudden change swept over me, making me realize that my fears were all a fabrication of lies from the greatest enemy of my soul. My heart was strengthened, all the clouds disappeared, and I felt it the greatest privilege of my life to confess the Lord Jesus by baptism before so large a congregation, no matter what the cost might be.

This was indeed a wonderful operation of the Holy Spirit upon my mind and heart, and I could not understand at the time how the change was effected, until Monday morning, when I received a letter from that well-known saint, Dr. Andrew A. Bonar, an aged pastor in Glasgow, saying: "My people and I were praying for you this morning at our service," and at the close of his letter he wrote that verse, "How beautiful are the feet of Him," etc., in Hebrew, for he was a Hebrew scholar. I have kept that letter unto this day as a remembrance of that servant of the Lord Jesus Christ.

Then I knew and understood that it was in answer to the prayers offered perhaps at the very moment I began to walk up the aisle, that Satan was defeated by the power of Jesus, who is the mighty God. The baptism had been announced in the papers and a rumor went abroad among the Jews that a rabbi was going to be baptized in the Barclay Church of Edinburgh. This angered them very much, and after they learned of the country and town from which I came, they wrote a letter to a prominent rabbi there, telling of my apostasy and inquiring what kind of an outcast I was, so that they might publish it in the papers that I was not anything more than a bad Jew and not worthy of any notice. Instead, the rabbi's

answer came, warning them against maligning such a
true and righteous Jew and that they should not believe
any evil reports about me, for I was a leader in Israel
whom they ought to respect. The head of the synagogue
and a few other Jews came to me with the letter and actually shed tears. They said, "The rabbis in your country
do not want to believe what you have done here, that
you publicly denounced Judaism and accepted the hated
religion of our enemies."

They began to plead with me, begging me to return to the Jewish faith. I then showed them from the
Scriptures that to believe in Jesus was Jewish faith, real
Jewish faith, and that they had no Jewish religion whatever if they did not believe in the Son of God. They were
struck with some Scriptures I quoted, and said: "We will
arrange for a meeting for you and our rabbi who knows
the Scriptures better than we do, and let him decide
whether you are right or not." They wanted me to meet
them in their own synagogue, but the pastor, Dr. Wilson, who baptized me, advised me not to go, as he
thought it dangerous; so the Jews hired a large private
hall and came to witness our argument.

THE LORD'S TRIUMPH

The hall was packed and in the middle was a small
table at which the rabbi and myself were seated. He began by hurling at me his fiery darts in the shape of hard,
puzzling questions and with great triumph ended the
first question, turning to the people all around and showing his ability in argument, and that it was a foregone

conclusion that this apostate could never answer him. But trusting in the Lord, I calmly and gently replied, so that disappointment was soon noticed upon his face. The answer was so direct that nearly everyone in the room could understand plainly. The meeting lasted for two hours, the pride of the rabbi subsiding gradually with every answer to his questions until at last he had no more to ask. Then all went away, disappointed and discouraged, not being willing at the time to admit that this apostate was right in his belief in Jesus, the Messiah. Later on, some of them did acknowledge the truth as it is in Jesus.

A DISTRESSING SILENCE

In the meantime, the silence of my dear wife caused me great pain. Not knowing the reason why she did not answer my letters (which I found afterwards had not been delivered to her), I suspected that she had given me up as dead on account of my coming to faith. Although at the time of my baptism I decided to follow the Lord Jesus even at the cost of losing wife and children and everything dear to me in the world, yet while the spirit was willing, the flesh became weak. Every day I looked for a letter from her and so she too was hoping to receive word from me, but both of us were greatly disappointed by hope deferred which made our hearts sick.

When I found myself alone, I would cry out, "Rose darling, are you alive? Why don't you write to me how you are and how our little ones are getting on?" There would come on spasm of terrible pain in the heart so that I thought I could not stand it. But the Lord Jesus to whom I carried all my woes was my strength. After a little talk with Him, my troubled heart was calmed and soothed. But my dear wife's suffering was worse as she did not have the comfort of a personal Saviour.

COMMUNICATION ESTABLISHED

About the beginning of August, a number of personal Christian friends in Edinburgh began to pray earnestly for a reunion of my family. Among the many friends the Lord gave me there, the most sympathetic and active, the most prayerful and Christ-like, was Miss Catherine G. Douglas, Lord Douglas' daughter, blessed be her memory. As a result of concerted prayers, the Lord began to work mightily. Soon the thought came that something wrong must have been done to our mutual letters, so I cabled my wife and to my great joy received a reply and subsequently arranged a different town from which she should mail and receive letters from me.

Thus were the schemes of our blind enemies defeated and we began to write long and frequent letters. She told all about the news that had come from America, announcing my apostasy which some believed and others did not. Mission work in that country is not known and no Jew has been converted to Christianity there. Besides, the Jews are superior to the so-called Christians there in civilization, in morality, in commerce and in politics, thus making it impossible to believe that a prominent Jew would stoop so low as to associate with such a degraded class of people. The reason that some believed the report concerning my conversion, was because it came from well-known Jews in America.

My wife could not believe such things and only asked me to tell her what made those Jews in America write such malicious letters about me. I wrote her that I talked too much about the Messiah, and when she came to me personally, I would tell her more fully. I could not say that the report was true and that I had become a Christian, because in the sense of the word Christian as she knew it, it was not true, and would have killed her affection for me forever. Thus, she began to think of coming to me. One day she went to a great rabbi, a miracle performer, and asked his advice. He told her not to believe the report but to go to me. Believing that the rabbi spoke through the Holy Spirit, she then and there decided to leave her country and relatives and join her husband in a strange place.

DETENTION OF MY WIFE

After she had written me that she had decided to come, deploring the sad fact that because of the Messiah I should have so many enemies, and expressing a hope that the Messiah would soon come and confer great honor upon me for all these persecutions, I gave thanks to God, and all my friends were glad to hear the news and praised the Lord for having answered prayers, expecting very soon to see her and the children. But a few days later she wrote that as soon as she had begun to prepare for the trip, her relatives opposed her leaving. One of her wealthy uncles said that he would spend half of his fortune, if necessary, to keep her and the children from me, for they too might be apostatized. He engaged a watchman, and prevented my wife's departure. This was a great disappointment, but my earnest friends were not discouraged and continued in fervent prayer to God.

I had corresponded previously with a number of my relatives who were much attached to me, explaining to them all about the Lord Jesus and His Messiahship. A nephew became especially interested and at last expressed his belief in Christ and continued corresponding with me in a very warm and affectionate way. Knowing I could trust him, I cabled him to arrange to take my wife and children by night and bring them to Berlin; and there another man sent by the friends from Edinburgh would bring them to Scotland.

Consequently, that nephew, an honest and experienced man, dealt wisely and assisted my wife and children after midnight when all was quiet and the watchman asleep. The Lord blessed his agency so that no harm befell them, and they reached Berlin in peace and safety. He notified me when they left town, and immediately a man was sent from Scotland to meet them.

In the morning when the watchman found what had happened, my wife's relatives tried to stop her by telegraphing the train officials all along the route which they supposed she took, to detain thieves, but fortunately they went a different way and thus escaped the trap laid for them.

ARRIVAL OF MY FAMILY

They were to arrive in Edinburgh at three o'clock

one morning, and Miss Douglas herself was so kind as to stay up to welcome them the minute they came. I anticipated great joy upon meeting my wife after so long an absence, but was greatly disappointed, for no sooner did she see me than she said, "Tell me first about the rumor of apostasy!" It was then my duty to explain my position as briefly as possible, so I said the Crucified One is our Messiah and that all the time I was searching for the Messiah I did not know that it was He, but now I have found it out and would show it to her from the Bible as soon as we had opportunity. That was enough to confirm the report and she turned away, crying, and said that in a day or two she would return with her children, as she could not stay, on account of my belief in the Crucified One whom she had learned from earliest childhood to hate and abhor.

For two days and two nights, she maintained the same position, not looking into my face or talking to me. I felt very sad about it, for whenever I tried to explain my belief she turned away and did not want to be in the same room; so I kept still, but continued in prayer to God.

HOW THE LORD AIDED

Our oldest boys of nine and seven respectively, were well educated for their age; they knew the Pentateuch and Psalms in Hebrew, well. So I read the second Psalm with them, showed that God spoke there of His Son and that He was the Messiah referred to in the second verse. I told them that this was the One in whom I believed and that through His death all our sins were forgiven and that He was sitting at the right hand of God, receiving our prayers and pleading for us. They, with childlike faith, accepted my teaching and joined me in prayer. This we did morning, noon and evening, and sometimes between these set hours. They too offered their short prayers, that the Lord would be merciful and lead their mother to accept this same Saviour and give her peace. She, from another room, was listening to our words, although we did not know it.

Two days later as I and the boys knelt in prayer, I suddenly felt her arm around me, and opening my eyes in surprise, I saw her smiling, though with tears in her eyes, while she said, "Do not worry, I will stay with you, for I see that you are the same child of God that you were. But I want you to promise to let me observe our religion as before. Then I will know that you are right." I agreed and we had a very happy hour; as the Lord showed His presence and gave us the peace that passeth understanding.

A HEBREW WOMAN'S STANDPOINT

It was hard to get Mrs. Cohn to read the Prophecies relating to the Messiah. According to Talmudic teaching, it is not right for parents to teach their daughters the law, that is, the Bible. Thus, Jewish women as a rule are kept in ignorance of the Word of God. While my dear wife was better educated than the average Jewess, she spoke several languages, was taught thoroughly the five books of Moses in the light of the Talmudic commentaries, and could read and write Hebrew, still she was brought up under the sentiment that a woman was not fit to study the prophets, especially with regard to such a mysterious and deep subject as that of the Messiah. She sympathized with me in my conviction, took an interest in my studies during my attendance at the New College of the Free Church of Scotland in Edinburgh, helped me different ways in my mission work among the Jews in Edinburgh and Glasgow, where I held meetings Friday evenings and Saturday afternoons, when I was free from College, but she did not want to search the Scriptures.

A WONDERFUL DREAM

However, two remarkable incidents, which stood out like two faithful witnesses, influenced her in a peculiar manner and impelled her to study and find out the truth for herself. One was that of a dream I had a few weeks before I sailed for America, when I had no thought of leaving my native country. In my dream I saw the sun rising in all its glory and brightness and not far from the sun were two moons, one very dark and the other full of light. As I looked at them with astonishment, lo and behold, the dark moon fell from the skies and disappeared, while the bright moon stayed there with the sun.

When I awoke, my heart was troubled and I told the dream to my wife. Later, in America, when I was led to see the truth as it is in Jesus, I at once recognized the interpretation of my dream. The moon is known by the Jews to be symbolic of the Hebrew race and their religion; for as the moon has the renewal of her light after darkness, so the Jews will be renewed in their national glory after their fall. The sun is symbolic of the Messiah who is called the Sun of righteousness. Thus, in that dream the Lord showed me that the dark side of my Jewish religion would disappear, while the real Jewish faith which is full of light would stay and abide with me through the Sun of righteousness, the Lord Jesus who is the light of the world. I used to write in my letters to my wife that "now I know what the puzzling dream meant, and when you come, I will tell you all about it." After her arrival at Edinburgh, I often referred to that dream and its interpretation which always impressed her very much.

THOUGHTS ON THE PASSOVER RITES

Another help to her was that of a thought the Lord gave me at the time when for her sake I observed the ceremony on the first Passover night after she reached Scotland. Among other sacred rites performed on the first night of the Passover feast are the following ones: Three cakes of unleavened bread [Ed. note: *matzoh*] are placed on the table, one above the other with a napkin between them so that each is separate from the other. The head of the family who is performing the ceremonies takes the middle cake and breaks it in halves, concealing one-half under the pillow of the lounge on which he reclines at that meal.

Reclining is a symbol of the freedom the Jews gained at the time when God brought them out from the bondage of Egypt. At certain intervals, four cups of wine are served to those seated at the table and at the third cup, the father takes out the half cake from between the pillows, and divides it among the family. I used to perform that ceremony year after year without considering the real reason for so doing, but with the light of the teaching of Messiah in my mind and heart, it suddenly dawned upon me what it all meant. The three cakes represent Father, Son and Holy Ghost; the middle one, the Son, broken in halves, indicates the body of the Son of God, broken for our sins. Concealing it under the pillow signifies the burial of the broken body, and bringing it fourth again at the third cup of wine indicates strikingly the resurrection of the Lord Jesus on the third day.

When the Lord gave me that thought, I at once with great joy in my heart, explained it to my dear wife and children, showing them that this custom which is being performed by all the Jews over the world from time immemorial, has in it the memory of death and resurrection of the Lord Jesus, and at the same time conveys to us His teaching of a triune God. The early disciples of the Lord Jesus were Jews and they must have instituted this ceremony among their people so that Messiah Yeshua (Jesus) should never be forgotten among them.

TRYING INCIDENTS
These thoughts startled my wife and she began to search the Scriptures and to talk to the Jews about the Lord Jesus, although she did not confess Him by baptism until two years later, but she could see the truth and she began to mention it in her letters to her broth-

ers and sisters in Europe. They became more bitter, and tried on one occasion to have the whole family extradited and brought back to Europe on some false charges. Mrs. Cohn's sister, who was very fond of her, enclosed in a letter a piece of black ribbon and said that this would show that she mourns her as dead.

This and many other annoying and harassing letters enervated her very much and affected her health, although she had always been strong and well. On several occasions, when I had to meet groups of Jews for debates, she accompanied me and talked to them in a most remarkable way. She had much wisdom and a winning and convincing way of conversation. Once a number of prominent Jewesses in Edinburgh visited and besought her with tears to leave me and stay with them. They offered her an amount of money and wanted to assure her by writing that she would never lack friends or means, if only she would stay among the Jews and give up her apostate husband. But she refused, and told them that she knew her husband better than they did and that she had more confidence in her husband than in all the Jews of Edinburgh. She also told them that they too ought to accept the Lord Jesus Christ.

RETURN TO NEW YORK

A year later an urgent call came to me from New York to go back and preach the Gospel to the Jews who persecuted me in that city. It was with great difficulty that I could accept. My dear wife did not wish to leave Scotland where we had very warm friends, from whom it was hard to separate and go again to a strange country, but some of our dearest friends there and some of the professors of the college brought their influence to bear upon us until Mrs. Cohn consented, and finally we reached New York, October, 1893. After having labored in New York for nearly a year, a call was extended to me from a Board in Toronto, to be their missionary to the Jews.

The Rev. John Wilkinson of London, who was at that time on a visit here, came to Toronto for the occasion, to inaugurate the Jewish mission there; but after I had been in the city for a week, holding meetings for the Jews, I was led, I believe of the Holy Spirit, not to accept the call, and so returned to New York. Soon after that, a Jewish friend took me for a visit to Brooklyn and on going across the river by ferry boat, I was surprised to see the large crowds of Jews accompanying us. I started a conversation with some of them and asked if they knew of any mission work being done in Brooklyn. They did not even seem to know what kind of a creature a missionary was.

Then a forcible thought came into my mind and heart that it was the place where the Lord wanted me to work. It came so suddenly that it made a tremendous impression upon me and I went home and told my dear wife the new thought that the Lord had given me and that I believed that it came to me directly from above. I had no rest day or night, for at meals and other times, that thought was always talking to me: "There is your place."

A NEW FIELD

While working in New York, the friends from Scotland liberally supported me as their missionary, but the minute I severed my connection with that mission, I had no prospect of any support. Mrs. Cohn used that as an argument against the thought of going to Brooklyn, but it did not convince me, and consequently, we moved to Brooklyn. Having no Christian friends in Brooklyn, nor as for that matter, in New York, for my time was filled with the work, I had great difficulty in deciding where to start the work and how to provide necessary means. One afternoon I went out from my house aimlessly and walked until I reached the then lately-founded Jewish colony in a suburb of Brooklyn, which is called to this day "Brownsville." There were no cars running there; the roads and streets were muddy; and not even sidewalks were laid at that time. A few houses were seen here and another group of houses there with only vacant lots between them. I felt impressed that I should rent a store there and begin holding meetings.

FIRST BROWNSVILLE MEETING

Just then I met a Jew with a pack of garments on his back hurrying across a vacant lot. I stopped and asked if he knew of a store for rent. As the Jew is always inquisitive, he queried why I wanted a store. I told him, "For a mission." He did not know what that was so I explained and told him about the Lord Jesus who can save him as well as all the Jews in Brownsville from their sins. There were some geese, chickens and a few goats on the vacant lots around us and I thought I was fulfilling the command "preach the Gospel to every creature" to the very letter. Then this man showed me a store not far away and I rented it. The following Saturday I held a meeting there and my acquaintance of a few days before was present. Seven other Jews came in and wanted to fight when they heard me mention the name of Jesus, but soon they became quiet and listened to the preaching of the Gospel with interest. Next Saturday, sixteen Jews attended the meeting, and next, many more. So the attendance kept on increasing until all the chairs were filled.

There was not a single Christian to help me in that pioneer work, financially or otherwise. During week days, I had the mission open daily for a reading room, while in the evenings, I taught the Jew English, by reading the New Testament in English with them. Thus I tried hard to make rapid progress by crowding a great deal into the short days which seemed to fly swiftly away, carrying with them so many Jewish souls without hope of salvation.

PERSECUTED BY MY BRETHREN

The leading Jews of Brownsville, seeing the continuous and steady attendance at the mission, became bitter and started to persecute me as well as the Jews who came in. Several times, attempts were made to do me bodily harm, but they only once succeeded in decoying and giving me a good beating. It was done as follows: One afternoon as I was leaving the reading room in charge of another, word was sent asking me to bring a Hebrew New Testament to a certain house. Being glad at the request, I hurried to the given address. No sooner had I finished my errand, than the Jew, the head of the house, a powerful man, fell upon me, knocked me down and battered me severely with his fists, jumped upon me with his feet and took me by the ears, raising my head and dropping me to the floor many times.

When he took hold of my ears, he repeated in Hebrew: "These ears which heard from Mount Sinai, 'Thou shalt not have other Gods beside me' and which now listen to the Christian god, must be pulled out of his head," emphasizing his words, "pulled out," by a terrible jerk at my ears. But when it was about unbearable, the Lord sent another Jew who came in unexpectedly and my tormentor was startled and stopped persecuting me.

So I gathered myself together and ran out as fast as I could. When I dragged myself home, my dear wife noticed the blood trickling down my face and was greatly shocked, but soon recovered and attended to my wounds, comforted and strengthened me in the Lord and in the blessed hope He gave us. She did not upbraid or triumph over me by saying, "Did I not tell you not to go Brooklyn?" A number of times, however, I heard her murmur with a deep sigh, "Oh, why was I so foolish as to leave Bonnie Scotland?" As a rule, she never complained under straitened circumstances, although she was brought up in wealth in her father's house where she never knew any need or want. Whenever I came home tired, she had a word of cheer, and with a heavenly smile on her face, always lightened my burdens.

THE LORD DOES PROVIDE

As I had nobody to help me financially when I opened the Mission, one month I had no money to pay the rent. When I told my dear wife about it, she immediately gave her last pieces of jewelry which she had as a remembrance from her mother who died before we were married, and said: "Pawn this and pay the Mission rent." I said to her that in case we had no money to redeem it, she would lose it and be sorry all her life. To this she replied: "If it is lost here, Jesus will return it to me in heaven." She must now have received it from the hand of the Saviour, for I never redeemed it for her here. I was determined not to ask money of any man for the work of the Lord. My thought was that since the Lord Jesus led me so wonderfully to Himself, giving me power enough to give up everything for His sake, I need not ask men for financial help, for He is able to give it to me in some way known to Him alone. And He did help me on several occasions in nothing short of miraculous ways, blessed be His holy name. One day when our children came home from school, there was only a cup of tea for their lunch. Upon explaining to them that there was no money to buy bread just now, one of the boys offered to go to the baker, who, he was sure, would give us a loaf of bread on credit. He went and returned without bread but with tears in his eyes; the baker refused to open an account with him and so hurt his feelings. Sadly disappointed, the children had to return to school without having a piece of bread with their tea. When I realized the situation that I as a father was not able to give bread

to my dear children, my heart nearly broke, and I has-
tened to my closet, shut the door, knelt down and wept
bitterly. Suddenly, the bell rang and the whistle of the
letter-carrier shrieked loud, and behold, there was a reg-
istered letter with money in it. It was the rent for my
dear wife's property, left her from her father, which she
entrusted to her brother in Hungary before she left for
Scotland. Her brother refused to send her the money for
the previous two years on account of her staying with
me. Now he sent it of his own accord. This was followed
by a letter from Mr. E. Rapahel, a Hebrew Christian in
Edinburgh, promising of his own free will, to send us
ten pounds monthly for a year. Mr. Raphael is of an excellent spirit and my dear wife used to call him, "a copy"
of Jesus. These things encouraged us greatly in our faith
in the Messiah and we thanked God.

HELP FROM CHRISTIAN FRIENDS

Soon after that, the Rev. T.J. Whitaker, pastor of
the Bushwick Avenue Baptist Church, raised in his own
church a monthly contribution to pay the rent of the
mission. The pastor was led in a peculiar way to this work.
He came to nearly every meeting and saw the progress
of the work. He told me later on, that he as well as many
other pastors, had never thought before of doing mission work among the Jews. When he realized its importance, he tried to help the cause in every way he could.
He used to sing for us in the meetings and the audience
enjoyed him very much. The Women's Auxiliary to the
City Mission heard somehow about the new movement

and they offered me a lady assistant who released me from teaching English in the evenings. Thus, I noticed that the Lord Jesus can accomplish many things without my asking help of men, and so I took courage and hoped for still greater blessings.

AN EARLY HARVEST

As good and as encouraging as these things were to me then, they were not to be compared with the great source of comfort to my soul which lay in the fact that the Jews began to believe in the Messiah. I used to meet Christian people at church and other places, from whom, when the subject of my occupation as missionary to the Jews was broached, I always heard discouraging utterances. One would say, "There is no use working among the Jews; they cannot come to faith," or "Yes, it is a waste of time," and so forth. Now I knew that this was only thoughtlessness on their part, for was not I a Jew and were not Paul and the other apostles Jews? I felt sure that the Gospel of the Lord Jesus has the same power today as yesterday, and over the Jew as well as over the Greek. But I thought that since the Jews have been shut out from the Gospel for so many centuries, it would take a long time to make them familiar with it and bring them to confess the Lord Jesus publicly.

I expected that my work would be only to sow the seed and some one else would reap. But, behold, after working for a few months, the Lord began to do wonderful things. Jews continued to come to the meetings in comparatively large numbers; those who were bitterly opposed became reconciled and some of them confessed the Lord Jesus as Messiah.

There was the case of an outspoken Jewish anarchist who used to come to the meetings, cursing, grinding his teeth and shaking his fist in my face, but before long, that man had to confess before the other Jews that there is no truth but in Jesus. There were several cases where two or three in a family came to faith and some whole families. There was the case of a Jewish lawyer who came to believe in Yeshua, his wife and his six children with him. He used to keep an open Bible on his desk, and when his clients came in, instead of talking business with them as usual, he called their attention to what he had found in the 53rd chapter of Isaiah and other passages, showing that Jesus is the Messiah. He was bitterly persecuted as a result of his confessions and had to leave Brownsville, for on one occasion, they attempted to set fire to his house.

Mrs. Cohn Used by God

Christian ministers as well as laymen began to rub their eyes and ask themselves: "What does it all mean?" Many Jews used to come to my house privately during the week to inquire more fully about the truth, for when they attended the meeting they could only listen. My dear wife used to take a great deal of pains explaining to these Jews, and told them of her own history. Nearly all those to whom she talked went away with strong faith in the living God and in His word about the Messiah. She soon gained the confidence of the Jewish men and women who had great respect for her tact, wisdom and godliness, as she grew stronger and stronger in the faith. Still, Satan put many temptations in her way to repel her from Messiah. For instance, our children who went to Sunday School, used to be persecuted by Christian children who called them names and sometimes tried to do them bodily harm. The children used to come home crying and tell their mama how the others called them names, but she, with true motherly love, took them in her lap and comforted them telling how the Lord Jesus suffered and how Elisha, the great prophet, was called names by a lot of children.

Thus, with great sorrow in her heart for the wounded feelings of her children, she knew how to comfort them and still remain steadfast in the Lord Jesus, from whom such things could not separate her.

TRIALS OF OUR CHILDREN

On one occasion a number of boys took one of my boys, who was only six or seven years at that time; they stretched him on the floor, some holding him down while another stepped on his legs below his knees and fractured them. In spite of the agonizing screams of the boy, they laughed and said, "That is the way the sheenies cry." Then the boy was brought home helpless and one can imagine what great grief and vexation that caused us, and I thought, "Now her faith will be weakened," for Jewish people used to come in and when they learned of it, say, "You see with whom you have to associate and who Christians are." But the warm heart of my dear wife never gave way, but always kept on saying: "And so they did to the prophets who had to suffer to glorify the name of Jehovah, and so must we." Our little boy was sick for a long time in the hospital, but the Lord healed him and our joy was made full. On a later occasion, however, some other so-called Christian children took one of our boys, and while several held him by force, another came with a knife and cut his lower lip through and through, and said: "This is the way we have to do with sheenies."

Many other trials came in different ways from the hands of so-called Christians, and I always felt worried lest they should repel either my dear wife or some of my children from the Messiah, but thanks be to God it was not so. All remained steadfast, heeding not such trials and persecutions, and after a short time, Mrs. Cohn was baptized by the Rev. W.C.P. Rhoades, D.D., pastor of the Marcy Avenue Baptist Church.

Further Assistance

We went on in the work under great financial difficulties for about two years, when the two Baptist societies, the Home Mission and the Church Extension, combined and offered their help. I looked upon this as a direct support from the Lord God in whom I trusted and to whom I looked for all my needs, for I did not apply to these societies, and yet they came so nobly and asked me if I wanted their aid. Of course, it was done in a natural way, but I did not know it. Rev. T.J. Whitaker, who used to come to the meetings, reported to the Baptist ministers and societies what he had witnessed and urged them to come and help.

So, one Saturday as I was preaching in Brownsville, about a dozen ministers and laymen surprised me by their presence. I told them that I would thankfully accept their support as I believed that the Lord sent them to my help, but I stipulated that I should not be interfered with in my methods of work in the spiritual dealings with my Jewish brethren whom I had studied from my earliest youth, knowing their characteristics, thoughts and daily life so well, and I also knew that Christian people had never studied Jewish life and consequently did not understand, humanly speaking, how to reach my brethren. I certainly believe, however, that God can use anybody, if He chooses, to work in a supernatural way. They agreed not to interfere with me and said they believed I was led by the Holy Spirit and that they would not come in between Him and the work, but would share in it by supporting it.

So they continued for eleven years, when I gratefully thanked them for their past kindness and resigned, as it became necessary to place the work upon an independent and interdenominational basis.

THE WILLIAMSBURG MISSION BEGUN

Now, at that time when these societies stepped in and one took upon itself the regular expenses of the Mission, about six hundred dollars a year, and the other offered to pay a thousand dollars a year as the missionary's salary, I saw that the Lord was indeed and in reality my loving Father and near Friend. So I said I would not give Him rest; I would ask still greater things. This little work that was done was only in Brownsville, where there were about 20,000 Jews at that time; but what was that little colony compared with the mass of Jews in another part of the city, in Williamsburg, an old Jewish settlement, then of about 50,000 Jews? Why not begin to do mission work there?

I went down to that neighborhood and on the first visit saw a very nice store, suitable for a mission. I asked for the rent; it was thirty dollars a month; but I did not have the money, and I also needed to buy chairs and to put up a platform, and arrange for gas. I counted that about fifty dollars was absolutely required to commence. I had a talk with the Lord in my private closet and then gave five dollars as a deposit on the rent, asking the landlord to wait two or three days, and if I did not bring him the rest, then the five dollars would be forfeited and he could rent the store to someone else.

Two days later, a friend told me that a lady who had dined with her recently, gave her a check for fifty-one dollars for the Jewish mission work. My friend had said that she knew of a rabbi who was doing mission work among the Jews, and the lady having never before contributed for Jewish mission work, wrote a check saying, "Give this to your Jewish friend." What joy it gave me that I could now rent that store and that the Lord had sent in the needed amount. The first time we opened it on a Friday evening, a crowd of Jews came to listen. Then the Lord raised up a friend and his wife, most lovely Christian characters, who have been paying the rent for that Mission, not by promise or pledge, but by mere choice, from month to month, until three years ago, when another friend began to share the expense with them.

JEWISH ANTAGONISM

As the crowds that came to the meetings grew larger and their interest in the Gospel became stronger, the Jewish leaders were bitter. They tried hard to stop the flow of men to the Mission, but could not prevail against the strong tide, driven by the Holy Spirit. Jews began to become convinced that Jesus is really the true Messiah. Some of them confessed Him publicly among other Jews and were greatly persecuted. Now and then zealots came to the meetings and in the midst of the sermon, would rise and cry out, "Fire!" and in this way succeeded in getting a large number out of the hall.

Once, these instigators gathered a crowd and came to the Mission, and at a given notice from their leader, began to upset chairs on which they sat, causing much confusion, and actually drove the people out of the meeting. They did this several times till I had to have a policeman, but even then they succeeded once in crowding him in the crush so that he was forced out in the crowd like a bullet from a gun. He fell down, lost his club and his hat. He was an Irishman and was greatly surprised that Jews could beat him so badly. However, the Lord gave me much patience to ignore these excitements, and I continued giving my testimony for Him, having had divine assurance that no evil shall befall those who trust in Him and co-labor with Him.

COMMENCEMENT OF OUR
SEWING SCHOOLS

Thus, a very busy time ensued. No help could be secured in the way of personal assistance in two active fields as interest in the evangelization of the Jews was almost non-existent among the dear Christian people. Just a few months before I opened the Williamsburg Mission, the Lord put it into my heart to gather children in the Brownsville Mission and work among them. I did not want to take them from the streets without their parents' knowledge as that would do much harm to the cause; so I went to those parents who attended the Mission and were somewhat interested in the Gospel and succeeded in getting thirteen girls to form a Sewing School.

Now, sewing was a branch of education which I had never pursued, but I thought through Messiah and for Him I could do anything; so I tried to teach the girls sewing. I met a Christian woman and asked if she would not come to help us teach in the Sewing School, but she said she could not go to Jewish children as the Jews are prejudiced and would not learn from a Christian or come to a mission. I told her that I had had one session and the children did come. "How many do you have?" she queried. "Thirteen for the first meeting," replied I. "Well," said she, "I would not come anyhow, because thirteen is a bad number to begin with." But soon the Lord raised up a few Christ-like women who came steadily and taught the girls sewing and the Gospel, especially two ladies who have been helping ever since that time and have not wearied in well-doing. The Lord is their reward.

The number of children began to increase from the beginning until there were as many as two hundred, so that often we could not find room or teachers for them. Reaching Jewish children is a very delicate matter. The children may see the truth in time, but as long as they are with their unbelieving parents, they dare not confess Him or speak about Him at home, as they highly respect them. The idea of their parents' supremacy is inborn. So even if we did not hear of many giving their heart to the Lord, their attendance at the meetings at least disarmed their prejudice and gave the girls a chance to learn about Messiah.

In this way, work among the children has been greatly blessed. There are now scores of mothers that, as girls, attended our Sewing School in the first two or three years, and they talk to their husbands about Messiah. Once, standing in a streetcar, hanging by a strap, I was surprised and embarrassed when a young woman, well dressed, rose and offered me her seat, calling me by name. I did not know her, but she was one of our Sewing School girls and remembered me very well and introduced me to her husband, saying: "This is the Rev. Mr. Cohn of whom I learned all that I told you."

PRACTICAL RESULTS

God's blessing has been continued on the work unto this day. Jews and Jewesses, young and old, have been led to confess the Lord Jesus and have begun to live different lives. One Jew told me that before he believed in Messiah, he tried to get rides without paying fare, but now he would never do such a thing. A woman testified that her husband had become a better man since he began to come to the Mission. Before that, he would never take her for a walk, but now he helps with the housework and when through, takes her and the baby out.

Time and space would not allow me to tell about the visible results that beyond my expectation I have been privileged to see. For fourteen long years crowds of Jews have continued to attend the meetings. Numbers of Jews continue to confess the Lord Jesus publicly, heeding not the great persecution to which they are exposed by their words. The most remarkable characteristic of the believers is that many of them are now preaching the Gospel to their own people in different towns. They have been gathered together and organized into a little church. Meetings for them especially are held every Monday evening, when nearly all speak, giving brief testimonies and thus strengthening one another's faith in the Lord Jesus. The Lord's Supper is partaken of by these brethren once every month.

USES OF OUR PAPER

The organ of the mission is a monthly paper called "The Chosen People," a sample copy of which can be had on application. It reports the progress of the work in both mission fields from month to month. The Lord, in His divine providence, has given us a large band of faithful friends who are indefatigably and untiringly praying for and supporting this Gospel work among

Jews, and all of them enjoy the paper greatly. They believe in the word of God, and therefore have the evangelization of the Jews deep in their hearts; we need many more such friends and you may rest assured that you will be most welcome to join this band of the faithful followers of the Lord Jesus. "Come thou with us and we will do thee good."

CLOSE OF MRS. COHN'S LIFE

My dear wife's illness which began soon after her arrival in Scotland, increased all the time. However, in all her weakness, through prayer and faith, she found His grace sufficient. With genuine self-denial her strong mother-heart forgot her own pain and thought for her dear children. Even when she lay in bed helpless sometimes at the point of death, she would whisper orders concerning the welfare of her children and the comfort of her husband. Not only was she the scriptural "virtuous woman" in the way of a good housewife and loving mother, but she also wonderfully combined these praiseworthy qualifications with the happy possession of a great missionary zeal.

She always managed to arrange her house affairs so as to be able to accompany me to the meetings, where her presence was an inspiration, like a light in a darkened room. Occasionally, she would address the audience and frequently talk personally to individual Jews about their souls at the close of the services pleading with them to accept the Lord Jesus as their Saviour. All respected her and many were led to

Messiah through her earnest testimony.

Sometimes she did visiting among the Jewesses upon whom Jewish tradition made it improper for me to call. Many Jewish women testified that she brought comfort to their sorrowing hearts and sunshine to their beclouded minds, and many Christian ladies who met and learned to love her said: "Your wife has been a blessing to me." All this, notwithstanding the fact that she was most of the time a sufferer. She never showed her illness no matter what pain she had to endure. Her face was always sunny and she ever rejoiced in the Lord, bearing her pain most patiently, even to the very end of her earthly life.

One of the messages she sent at the last was: "Tell the children to submit to God's will." Her heart and mind were always firmly fixed upon the Lord Jesus, her Saviour. Once, while suffering much pain, she asked me a few questions as to the position of the Lord Jesus in heaven. After my answer, she said: "My thoughts are continually wandering away from me, up and up, far yonder they break through that mysterious wall and show me how I will meet Jesus there. My mind pictures Him as sitting on a great white throne, holding out a golden scepter as Ahasuerus did to Esther the Queen." These as well as a number of other utterances, from her feverish lips during her last hours, revealed her absolute faith in the love, mercy and truth of the Lord Jesus who promised to receive His followers into the prepared place; she never doubted, but could see her way clear and straight to the presence of the King of kings without any fear whatever.

Such words could not but confirm my conviction that there has not been a more devoted Christian woman on earth. She was anxiously waiting to see the much needed building for the mission realized. She used to join me in a private prayer to God to move upon the hearts of those dear Christians who have the means and cause them to put up the building. She was so sanguine and confident that she never doubted its realization. However, toward the end of her life when very feeble, she said to me: "I have been pulling with you hard uphill for so many years, waiting for the Mission building and now when almost to the top, the Lord wants me to go away. I have asked God to let me live to see the building and a messianic congregation worshipping the Lord in it, but He says no, just as to Moses when he wanted to enter the Promised Land."

Mrs. Cohn was greatly rejoiced every time a Jew, or a Jewess confessed Jesus as the Messiah. Her happiest days in America, she told me once, were those when she assisted at the immersions of new believers. She was hoping to see a large movement among the Jews toward Messiah, and thus a few hours before her departure, though too weak to move, her missionary spirit rose above her sufferings and everything dear to her heart on earth and she expressed the desire to get up and "go down on my knees and die praying, so that my soul may go up there with a special petition for the speedy conversion of my people."

Mrs. Cohn's last illness began in August, 1907. After a request for prayer on her behalf made in the

March, 1908, *Chosen People*, her critical condition changed so that there was hope for her recovery, several serious symptoms disappearing one after another, almost in a supernatural way. She, herself, however, realized all this time, that she was going to leave us and hinted as much, though avoiding plainer talk for fear it might distress me. Thus, at the end of two weeks she suddenly began to fail, and in two days slipped away.

Saturday morning, April 4th, at 9:30, she began to lose consciousness and at 11:30 she breathed her last. A number of friends, even from out of town, were so kind and came to comfort us. Some Jews who were not yet believers but who had heard Mrs. Cohn's short talks in the Mission expressed in writing and personally their great sorrow and deep sympathy. On Monday evening, the funeral service was held in our home. The Rev. W.C.P. Rhoades, D.D., her pastor, who had baptized her twelve years ago, delivered an impressive address. Thus ended a life which was a continuous and effective testimony for the Lord Jesus. And yet, not ended; for she: "though dead, yet speaketh"; speaketh to my heart, and to the hearts of those who knew and loved her, both among Jew and Gentile. For me, who am now left alone to complete the work for which we both sowed in tears, she will ever live, a constant inspiration and motive power in the carrying on of the work which was the supreme love of her life; until I, too, shall reach the yonder shore, and amidst the glad meeting and greeting, we both hear the "well done, thou good and faithful servant."

A FINAL WORD

In loving appreciation and gratitude to God for such a life and such an inspiration, I have written these pages, in the hope that the Lord will use them to the blessing and encouragement of many souls, and to the awakening of an unprecedented interest in Israel.

Amen. ∞

About CHOSEN PEOPLE MINISTRIES, INC.

CHOSEN PEOPLE MINISTRIES, INC. (CPM) (formerly ABMJ—AMERICAN BOARD OF MISSIONS TO THE JEWS), was raised up by God as an arm of the local church to bring the Gospel to the Jewish people. It is an independent work supported by thousands of individual contributors and churches.

OUR MINISTRIES

יֵשׁוּעַ

It is our specific ministry to preach the Gospel of Yeshua, the Messiah, and to show our Lord's love to the Jewish people throughout the world. A direct and sustained witness is carried out by the following means:

❋ Establishing Messianic congregations.

❋ Holding fellowship meetings, Bible studies, worship services, and doing personal work. Each worker is trained and able to lead home discussion groups and provide home instruction for inquirers. We emphasize returning to the God of Israel through faith in the finished work of *Yeshua haMashiach* (Jesus the Messiah) for the forgiveness of sin so that one might enter into the spiritual blessings promised to the Jews. Our workers are also trained to present the relationship between the Old and New Covenants.

❋ Employing canvassing techniques. This work is done through telephone calls and personal door-to-door approach.

❋   Helping churches relate to the Jewish people and thereby increasing the witness to them. This is done through the following methods:

Monthly publishing of *The Chosen People* newsletter, a periodical for Christians with news of interest regarding Jews, our work among them, Jewish customs and traditions, and an interpretation of contemporary events. This informative and insightful magazine will keep you abreast of the world of Jewish missions and evangelism. You will be blessed as you read the testimonies of Jewish people who have accepted Yeshua as their Messiah and Savior.

Presentations explaining our work and special programs geared to inform Christians about the prophetic significance of some Jewish holidays, and so forth.

Distributing an extensive variety of books and tracts, as well as audio and video tapes.

Producing special radio and TV broadcasts designed to provide a witness to the Jewish community and to provide insight and instruction to Christians; our TV programs are most often aired during Jewish holidays.

Special ministry to children and young people. Each of our congregations has classes for small children and teenagers. Most have some kind of thrust toward college students. Each year our congregations conduct a camp for children and teenagers.

Volunteer programs for laypersons interested in direct involvement with CHOSEN PEOPLE MINISTRIES.

OUR BELIEFS

All workers and Board members of CHOSEN PEOPLE MINISTRIES must subscribe to doctrines fundamental to the faith. We declare and affirm our belief in the following:

❋   The Divine inspiration, infallibility, and authority of both the Old and New Covenants

❋   The Triune God and the Deity of the Lord Jesus (Yeshua) as the only begotten Son of God, and the promised Messiah

❋   His sacrificial blood atonement at Calvary, His bodily resurrection from the dead, and His premillennial second coming

❋   The necessity of presenting the Gospel to the Jewish people.

The present emphasis of CHOSEN PEOPLE MINISTRIES is on expanding the work among the Jewish people in large urban areas. CHOSEN PEOPLE MINISTRIES also continues active works in Israel, Canada, South America, Kiev and Germany, and is planning, by the grace of God, to establish effective outreaches in the 11 countries where 94% of the world's Jewish population will live by the year 2000.

As an arm of the local church to the Jewish community, CHOSEN PEOPLE MINISTRIES cannot function independently of the rest of the Body (the Church at large). We need your help. Paul reminds us that it is the responsibility of the Church to share the Gospel with Jewish people (Romans 1:16, 17).

How would you answer this question: "What have I done for the Jewish people, considering what they have done for me?" It was through the Jews that our Messiah, the Lord Jesus, came. It was through the Jews that our Scriptures were given. It is to the Jews that our Messiah will return (Zechariah 12:10). Shouldn't they have the same opportunity to hear the Gospel as the Gentiles? With your prayers and financial support, together we can reach the Jewish people.

OUR PROMISE TO YOU

As an organization dating from 1894, we can make you a promise that we have made and kept through over 100 years of ministry. We promise that your name and address will never be sold, traded, or given to any other organization or individual. Our mailing lists remain strictly confidential.

As a supporter of this ministry you will receive our monthly publication, *The Chosen People* newsletter. You will also receive a monthly prayer letter stating our needs and giving you the opportunity to contribute to a particular worker or project. You will also receive a thank you letter and receipt for every gift you give. From time to time the missionaries whom you support through our organization will share personally with you and will send you praise and progress reports concerning their particular work, asking you to pray for specific needs.

As a Charter Member of the ECFA (the Evangelical Council for Financial Accountability), we are committed to having outside auditors publish our financial statements. In Canada we are members of the CCCC (Canadian for Christian Charities), the Canadian affiliate of the ECFA. Upon request, you may receive a copy of their statement and full financial disclosure.

Additional Reading

JEWISH HISTORY

Allegro, John M. *The Chosen People.* Garden City, N.Y.: Doubleday, 1972. A study of Jewish history from the exile until the Bar-Kokhba revolt (sixth century B.C. to second century A.D.). The author discusses the question: "Did the Babylonian Jew lay the foundation of anti-Semitism by originating the doctrine of the 'Chosen Race'?"

Ben-Sasson, H.H., ed. *A History of the Jewish People.* Cambridge, Mass.: Harvard Univ. Press, 1976.

Blau, Joseph L., and Salo W. Baron, eds. *The Jews of the United States, 1790–1840* (3 vols.). New York: Columbia Univ. Press, 1963. Contains materials from primary sources. Provides an understanding of the first days of Jewish experience in the United States and changes in Jewish life brought about by this experience. Includes chronological lists of documents. 955 pages.

Cohen, Shaye J.D. *From the Macabees to the Mishna.* In Wayne A. Meeks, ed., Library of Early Christianity (Vol. 7). Philadelphia: Westminster Press, 1987.

Dimont, Max. *The Jews, God, and History.* New York: Signet Books, 1962. A very basic history but well written and interesting. Good index. 421 pages. Ebban, Abba. *My People.* New York: Random House, 1968. A history of the Jews, written as an epic drama. Excellent photographs.

Elbogen, Ismar. *A Century of Jewish Life.* Jewish Publication Society of America, 1944. Written with the primary intent of bringing up-to-date the history in Heinrich Graetz's six-volume *History of the Jews.* Helpful bibliography. 682 pages.

Finkelstein, Louis, ed. *The Jews: Their History, Their Role in Civilization, Their Religion and Culture* (3 vols.). New York: Schocken Books, 1971. Written by the chancellor of the Jewish Theological Seminary of America. A complete intellectual account of Jewish life and thought.

Fleming, Gerald. *Hitler and the Final Solution.* Berkeley, Calif.: Univ. of California Press, 1982.

Gade, Richard E. *A Historical Survey of Anti-Semitism.* Grand Rapids, Mich.: Baker Book House, n.d.

Gilbert, Martin. *Atlas of the Holocaust.* Jerusalem: Steimatsky's Agency, 1982.

———. *The Holocaust: A History of the Jews of Europe During the Second World War.* New York: Holt, Rinehart and Winston, 1985.

———. *Jewish History Atlas.* New York: Macmillan, 1969.

Goldwurm, Hirsch, ed. *History of the Jewish People: The Second Temple Era.* New York: Mesorah Publications, 1983.

Golub, Jacob S. *In the Days of the Second Temple.* New York: Union of American Hebrew Congregations, 1929. Especially useful for young readers.

Graetz, Heinrich. *History of the Jews* (originally Geschichte Grayzel, Solomon. *A History of the Contemporary Jew: 1900 to Present.* New York: Atheneum, 1972. Written by a past professor of Jewish history at Gratz College. Concise. Useful bibliography. 179 pages.

Hull, William L. *The Fall and Rise of Israel: The Story of the Jewish People During Their Dispersal and Regathering.* Grand Rapids, Mich.: Zondervan, 1954. An excellent discussion of the subject.

Josephus, Flavias. *The Jewish War.* Gaalya Cornfeld and Paul L. Maier, eds. Grand Rapids, Mich.: Zondervan, 1982. Extensive commentary and archaeological illustrations.

—————. *The Life and Works of Josephus.* John C. Whiston, trans. Grand Rapids, Mich.: Associated Publishers and Authors, n.d. Jewish historian of the Jewish wars with Rome and so forth.

Margolis, Max L., and Alexander Marx. *A History of the Jewish People.* Philadelphia: World Publishing Co., 1958. Margolis was editor-in-chief of the Bible translation published by the Jewish Publication Society. Marx was professor of history at the Jewish Theological Seminary of America. An historical account of Judaism and Judaic thought. Excellent bibliography. 737 pages.

Mitscherlich, Alexander, and Fred Mielke. *Doctors of*

Infamy. Henry Schuman, 1949. The head of the German Medical Commission to Military Tribunal No. 1, Nuremberg, describes Nazi atrocities.

Morse, Arthur D. *While Six Million Died*. New York: Random House, 1968. Describes America's indifference to the Jews of the Holocaust.

Rausch, David A. *A Legacy of Hatred*. Chicago: Moody Press, 1984.

Rivkin, Ellis. *The Shaping of Jewish History*. New York: Charles Scribner's Sons, 1971. Written by a professor of Jewish history at Hebrew Union College. A radically economic approach, providing valuable insights into the Pharisaic "revolution" in Judaism especially. Provocative and thoughtful.

Roth, Cecil. *A History of the Marranos*. Philadelphia: Jewish Publication Society, 1960. Writer was professor in Jewish Studies at Oxford University, England. Comprehensive account of forced conversions of Jews in Spain, and of the converts. 375 pages.

Sachar, Abram Leon. *A History of the Jews*. New York: Alfred A. Knopf, 1964. Written by a president of Brandeis University. Good bibliography and index. Comprehensive treatment of "thirty centuries of Judaism." One of the better one-volume histories.

Sachar, Howard M. *Diaspora: An Inquiry into the Contemporary Jewish World*. New York: Harper and Row, 1985.

St. John, Robert. *Tongue of the Prophets*. North Hollywood, Calif.: Wilshire Book Co., 1952. A biography of Eliezer Ben-Yehuda, the father of modern Hebrew.

Scholem, Gershom. *Origins of the Kabbalah.* Princeton, N.J.: Princeton Univ. Press, 1987.

———. *Sabbatai Zevi: The Mystical Messiah* (Bollingen Series XCIII). Princeton, N.J.: Princeton Univ. Press, 1973.

Shenker, Israel. *Coat of Many Colors: Pages from Jewish Life.* Garden City, N.Y.: Doubleday, 1985.

Siegel, Richard, and Carl Rheius. *The Jewish Almanac.* New York: Bantam Books, 1980. A fact-filled book on the traditions, history, religion, wisdom, and achievements of the Jewish people.

Silberman, Charles E. *A Certain People.* New York: Summit Books, 1985.

Wyman, David S. *The Abandonment of the Jews: America and the Holocaust, 1941-1945.* New York: Pantheon Books, 1984.

Zeitlin, Solomon. *The Rise and Fall of the Judean State* (2 vols.). Philadelphia: Jewish Publication Society of America, 1967. Written by the professor of Rabbinic Law and Lore at Dropsie College. An account of the political, social, economic, and religious events of the second Jewish Commonwealth.

MODERN ISRAELI HISTORY

Antonius, George. *The Arab Awakening.* Toms River, N.J.: Capricorn Books, 1965. The most comprehensive and important work on Arab nationalism. 412 pages.

Ben-Gurion, David. *Israel.* Tel Aviv: Sabra Books, 1972. A very personal and often autobiographical history of the nation which the author helped to create.

Bright, John. *History of Israel* (3rd ed.). Philadelphia: Westminster Press, 1981.

Collins, Larry, and Dominique LaPierre. *O Jerusalem.* New York: Simon and Schuster, 1972. Well-written account of the events of 1948 from various perspectives. 657 pages.

Gilbert, Martin. *The Arab Israeli Conflict: Its History in Maps.* London: Weidenfeld and Nicolson, 1979.

Hertzberg, Arthur, ed. *The Zionist Idea.* New York: Atheneum, 1969. History contained in introduction. Source materials from 1790s to formation of Jewish state. Contains writings of the intellectuals of Zionism. With biographies. 619 pages.

Katz, Samuel. *Battleground: Fact and Fantasy in Palestine.* New York: Bantam Books, 1973. A well-documented history of the conflict between the Arabs and Israel from 1948. Somewhat pro-Israel. 239 pages.

Luttwak, Edward, and Dan Horowitz. *The Israeli Army.* New York: Harper and Row, 1975. How was the army created in a single generation from a people who had no army for several thousand years?

Peters, Joan. *From Time Immemorial: The Origins of the Arab Jewish Conflict Over Palestine.* New York: Harper and Row, 1984.

Sachar, Howard M. *A History of Israel.* New York: Alfred A. Knopf, 1976.

Segal, Ronald. *Whose Jerusalem?* New York: Bantam Books, 1973. A discussion of the possibilities for war and peace in the Middle East, with consideration being given to the personalities involved.

Shipler, David K. *Arab and Jew: Wounded Spirits in a Promised Land.* New York: Times Books, 1986.

Silverberg, Robert. *If I Forget Thee O Jerusalem.* New York: William Morrow, 1970. Presents a complete picture of the nature and construction of the state of Israel as it relates to American Jews. 611 pages.

Weizmann, Chaim. *Trial and Error* (2 vols.). Philadelphia: Jewish Publication Society of America, 1949. Biographical account of Zionism by Israel's first president; biased, but interesting.

JEWISH THEOLOGY AND TRADITION

Cohen, A., ed. *The Soncino Chumash.* New York: Soncino Press, 1970. The five books of Moses with Haftarah. Hebrew text with English translation and an exposition based on classical Jewish commentaries. Good index. 1,200 pages.

Commentary Magazine, eds. *Condition of Jewish Belief* Northvale, N.J.: Jason Aronson, 1989. A symposium of thought on the basic topics of Judaism from the full spectrum of the rabbinate. 280 pages.

Eisendrath, Maurice N. *Can Faith Survive?* New York: McGraw-Hill, 1964. Written by a president of the Union of American Hebrew Congregations and leader of Reform Jewry. A redefinition of Jewish values and a rededication to them. Interesting.

Ganzfried, Solomon. *Kitzur Schulchan Aruch* (Code of

Jewish Law). New York: Hebrew Publishing, 1961. A compilation of the rules and precepts which have governed Jewish life for centuries. Detailed. A final authority on matters of Jewish law and custom. Invaluable for understanding of Jewish traditions and orthodoxy. 562 pages.

Gaster, Theodore H. *Festivals of the Jewish Year: A Modern Interpretation and Guide.* New York: William Morrow, 1953.

Glazer, Nathan. *American Judaism* (2nd ed.). Chicago: Univ. of Chicago Press, 1972. Written by a professor of Sociology at University of California, Berkeley. Concerns Jewish identity, immigration to the United States, and the outlook of Jews today with regard to social and religious needs. 149 pages.

Herberg, Will. *Judaism and the Modern Man.* Philadelphia: Jewish Publication Society of America, 1959. Discusses the question: "How relevant is Judaism to life today?" 310 pages.

Heschel, Abraham. *The Sabbath.* New York: Farrar, Straus and Giroux, 1975.

Idelsohn, A.Z. *Jewish Liturgy.* New York: Schocken Books, 1932. An excellent resource for a study of ritual, music, and liturgy in Judaism by a scholar in this field.

Jacobs, Louis. *Principles of the Jewish Faith.* Northvale, N.J.: Jason Aronson, 1988.

Kaplan, Mordecai M. *Judaism as a Civilization.* New York: Schocken Books, 1967. Reconstructionist Judaism discussed by its founder. 522 pages.

————. *The Meaning of God in Modern Jewish Religion.* Reconstructionist Press, 1962. Interpretation of Reconstructionism. 368 pages.

Kertzer, Morris N. *What Is a Jew?* New York: Macmillan, 1960. Written by the rabbi of a large temple in New York State. A brief account of the religious practices of the reform tradition of Judaism. 179 pages.

Kitov, A.E. *The Jew and His Home.* New York: Shengold Publishers, 1973. A very informative description of the traditional view of daily life in a Jewish home.

Kolatch, Alfred J. *Who's Who in the Talmud.* New York: Jonathan David Publishers, 1964.

Landman, Isaac, ed. *The Universal Jewish Encyclopedia* (10 vols.). University Jewish Encyclopedia Co., 1948. An excellent source of information for those who desire extensive materials.

Landman, L., ed. *Messianism in the Talmudic Era.* Hoboken, N.J.: Ktav Publishing House, 1979.

Levi, Isaac. *The Synagogue: Its History and Function.* London: Valentine Mitchell, 1963.

Menkus, Belden, ed. *Meet the American Jew.* Nashville, Tenn.: Broadman Press, 1963. Compiled primarily for Christians by Jews for the Southern Baptist Church. Very basic, but useful.

Moore, George Foot. *Judaism in the First Centuries of the Christian Era* (3 vols.). Cambridge, Mass.: Cambridge University Press, 1948. Written by a non-Jewish Harvard University professor of the history of religion. Offers considerable depth of information on the subject of Rabbinic Judaism and the Talmud and is considered perhaps the best work of its kind.

Rabinowicz, Rabbi Tzvi. *A Guide to Life: Jewish Laws and Customs of Mourning.* Northvale, N.J.: Jason Aronson, 1989.

Sandmel, Samuel. *We Jews and Jesus.* New York: Oxford Univ. Press, 1965. Written by professor of Bible and Hellenistic Literature at Hebrew Union College. A review of Jewish attitudes toward Jesus and Christianity with explanations from an historical perspective. 153 pages.

Schauss, Hayyim. *The Jewish Festivals from Their Beginnings to Our Own Day.* New York: Union of American Hebrew Congregations, 1965.

Shulman, Albert M. *Gateway to Judaism* (2 vols.). New York: Thomas Yoseloff Publishers, 1971. Concise encyclopedia of Jewish thought and life (including doctrines of Judaism, ceremonies, literature, and so forth). Written in a readable form and organized and divided into chapters. Obviously not comprehensive, but useful for those not desirous of obtaining a more extensive work.

Siegel, Richard, Michael Strassfeld, and Sharon Strassfeld. *The First Jewish Catalog.* Philadelphia: Jewish Publication Society of America, 1973.

Sloti, Judah J., ed. *The Soncino Talmud* (18 vols.). London: Soncino Press, 1952.

Strassfeld, Michael. The Jewish Holidays: *A Guide and Commentary.* New York: Harper and Row, 1985.

Syme, Daniel P. *The Jewish Home: A Guide for Jewish Living.* Northvale, N.J.: Jason Aronson, 1989.

Weiner, Herbert. *9 1/2 Mystics.* New York: Macmillan/ Collier Books, 1969. An interesting "modern" account of Jewish mysticism.

Wiesel, Elie. *Souls on Fire.* New York: Random House, 1972. Biographical sketches and legendary accounts of Chasidic masters.

Zohar, The. Harry Sperling and Maurice Simon, trans. London: Soncino Press, 1933. A form of commentary on the mystical meaning of the Pentateuch. Originally written in Aramaic and Hebrew. Purportedly written by Rabbi Simeon ben Yohai, second century A.D.

JEWISH FOLKLORE AND FICTION

Aleichem, Sholom. *Collected Stories of Sholom Aleichem* (2 vols.). New York: Crown Publishers, 1946. Stories of the Old Country which have become part of Jewish culture. "Fiddler on the Roof" is taken from this collection. 689 pages.

Ausubel, Nathan, ed. *A Treasury of Jewish Folklore.* New York: Crown Publishers, 1948. For an understanding of Jewish tradition, superstition, and folk culture, this is invaluable. Glossary. 734 pages.

———. *A Treasury of Jewish Humor.* New York: Paperback Library, 1967. Interesting and enjoyable—the flavor of Jewish culture. 760 pages.

Bellow, Saul, ed. *Great Jewish Short Stories.* Laurel, Md.:

Dell Publications, 1963. A collection of stories from Europe and America. 414 pages.

Feuer, Leon I. *Jewish Literature Since the Bible* (2 vols.). New York: Union of American Hebrew Congregations, 1937. A collection of Jewish writings from the "Apocrypha."

Glatzer, Nahum N., ed. *Hammer on the Rock: A Midrash Reader.* Wisdom and Poetry of the Talmud and Midrash. New York: Schocken books, 1975.

Golden, Harry. *You're Entitle'.* Greenwich, Conn.: Fawcett Press, 1962. Other volumes by author are *Enjoy, Enjoy; Only in America; For 2 Cents Plain.* A leading Jewish humorist writes about Jewish life and experience in the United States.

Greenburg, Sidney. *A Modern Treasury of Jewish Thought.* New York: Thomas Yoseloff Publishers, 1960.

Keston, Hermann, ed. *Heinrich Heine: Works of Prose.* New York: L.B. Fisher, 1943.

Lewis, Sinclair. *It Can't Happen Here.* Garden City, N.Y.: Doubleday, 1935. As the events in Germany confronted the world, Americans declared that mass murder, death chambers, and the nightmare which Hitler created could never take place in our "free" society. Lewis relates American temperament and culture to that of Germans and, in this novel, poses interesting questions.

Michener, James A. *The Source.* New York: Fawcett Crest, 1984. A novel-form "history of Israel" using archaeology to move the setting from one period to the next. Many inaccuracies.

Nahmad, H.M., ed. *A Portion in Paradise and Other Jewish Folktales.* New York: Schocken Books, 1974. Fascinating legends, and so forth.

Newman, Louis. *The Hasidic Anthology.* Northvale, N.J.: Jason Aronson, 1987.

Potok, Chaim. *The Chosen.* New York: Fawcett Crest, 1965. Written by a rabbi who was editor of the Jewish Publication Society of America. An attempt to describe Chasidic and Orthodox Judaism in the form of a novel. Provides the reader with a feeling for the subject—makes Chasidism, especially, more understandable. 350 pages.

———. *The Promise.* New York: Fawcett Crest, 1969. Same description as for The Chosen. 350 pages.

———. *My Name is Asher Lev.* New York: Fawcett Crest, 1972. Same description as for *The Chosen.* 350 pages.

Rosten, Leo. *The Joys of Yiddish.* New York: Pocket Books, 1970.

———. *Treasury of Jewish Quotations.* New York: McGraw-Hill, 1972.

Steinsaltz, Adin. *The Essential Talmud.* New York: Basic Books, 1976.

Vilnay, Zev. *Legends of Jerusalem.* Philadelphia: Jewish Publication Society of America, 1977.

———. *Legends of Judea and Samaria.* Philadelphia: Jewish Publication Society of America, 1977.

Waxman, Meyer. *History of Jewish Literature: From the Close of the Bible to Our Own Day.* New York: Bloch Publishing, 1936.

ARCHAEOLOGY

Albright, W.F. *The Archeology of Palestine.* New York: Pelican, 1949. An archaeological survey of the peoples and cultures of this area. Albright was one of the world's leading archaeologists.

Baez-Camargo, Goncalo. *Archaeological Commentary on the Bible.* Garden City, N.Y.: Doubleday/Galilee Books, 1986.

Baney, Ralph E. *Search for Sodom and Gomorrah.* Hortonville, Wisc.: CAM Press, 1962. Interesting facts about the Dead Sea.

Ben-Dov, Meir. *In the Shadow of the Temple: The Discovery of Ancient Jerusalem.* New York: Harper and Row, 1982.

Bowen, Barbara M. *Through Bowen Museum with Bible in Hand.* Grand Rapids, Mich.: Eerdmans, 1946. Offers archaeology facts which explain many Biblical expressions and Israelite customs.

Burrows, Millar. *The Dead Sea Scrolls.* New York: Viking, 1955. An account of the most important archaeological discovery of modern times, with "translations of the principal scrolls and a study of their contributions to our understanding of Biblical times." Author was a Yale professor.

Cross, Frank Moore, Jr. *The Ancient Library of Qumran.* Garden City, N.Y.: Doubleday/Anchor Books, 1961. Author is considered to be a top authority in this field. "A comprehensive study of the Dead Sea Scrolls and the community which owned them." Very readable. 243 pages.

Davis, George T.B. *Bible Prophecies Fulfilled Today.* New York: Million Testaments Campaigns, 1951. Good background material.

————. *Fulfilled Prophecies That Prove the Bible.* New York: Million Testaments Campaigns, 1931. Good background material.

Finegan, Jack. *Light from the Ancient Past.* Princeton, N.J.: Princeton Univ. Press, 1949. Archaeological background of Judaism (and Christianity). Very useful.

Free, Joseph P. *Archeology and Bible History.* Wheaton, Ill.: Scripture Press, 1972. Biblical criticism answered and explained by archaeological discoveries.

Jidejian, Nina. *Tyre Through the Ages.* Dar El-Mashreq, 1969. Excellent description of Tyre, Sidon, and other ancient cities.

Layard, Austen. *Discoveries Among the Ruins of Ninevah and Babylon.* New York: Harper and Brothers, 1853. An interesting account of the archaeological findings in these two ancient capitals.

Mare, Harold W. *Archaeology of the Jerusalem Area.* Grand Rapids, Mich.: Baker Book House, 1987.

Robinson, George L. *Sarcophagus of an Ancient Civilization.* New York: Macmillan, 1930. History and archaeological material on such places as Petra, Edom, and Israel. Excellent.

Wright, Thomas. *Early Travels in Palestine.* Henry G. Bohn, 1948.

Yadin, Yigael. *Bar-Kokhba: The Rediscovery of the Legendary Hero of the Second Jewish Revolt Against Rome.*

New York: Random House, 1971. Archaeological account of the second Jewish revolt against Rome and its leader, Bar-Kokhba. Based on discoveries by the author (one of Israel's leading archaeologists) made in the early 1970s.

———. *Hazor: The Rediscovery of the Great Citadel of the Bible.* New York: Random House, 1975.

———. *Masada: Herod's Fortress and the Zealots' Last Stand.* New York: Random House, 1966. Masada archaeological expedition, Hebrew University, Jerusalem. Has excellent photos of the archaeological work at Masada, the last holdout of the Jewish people against the Romans.

———. *The Temple Scroll.* London: Weidenfeld and Nicholson, 1985.

JEWISH PHILOSOPHY

Agus, J.B. *The Evolution of Jewish Thought.* New York: Harper and Row/Abelard-Schuman, 1959.

Buber, Martin. *Kingship of God.* New York: Harper and Row, 1967.

———. *Moses: The Revelation and the Covenant.* New York: Harper and Brothers, 1958.

Heschel, Abraham. *Between Man and God.* New York: Harper and Brothers, 1959.

———. *Man Is Not Alone.* Farrar, Straus and Giroux, 1952.

———. *Man's Quest for God.* New York: Charles Scribner's Sons, 1954.

Maimonides, Moses. *Guide for the Perplexed*. M. Fried-
lander, trans. London: Pardes Publishing House,
1904. Maimonides is one of the two most signifi-
cant Jewish philosophers and theologians of the
Medieval Period. His spiritual wisdom has been
appreciated by Jews and non-Jews alike.

———. *Mishnah Torah*. Philip Birnbaum, ed. New York:
Hebrew Publishing Co., 1967.

Mendelssohn, Moses. *Jerusalem: And Other Jewish Writings*. New York: Schocken Books, 1969. Mendelssohn,
grandfather of composer Felix Mendelssohn, was a
remarkable man and a scholar of great culture. He
was held in high esteem by the most important
people of his day and contributed much to the even-
tual emancipation of the Jewish people in Germany.

Runes, Dagobert D., ed. *The Hebrew Impact on Western
Civilization*. New York: Philosophical Library, 1951.
Offers a comprehensive and factual account of the
Jewish contributions to Western culture and society.
875 pages.

Wouk, Herman. *This Is My God*. Garden City, N.Y.:
Doubleday, 1961. A personal exploration of the
Jewish relationship to, and understanding of, God.

Yaffe, James. *The American Jews: Portrait of a Split
Personality*. New York: Random House, 1968.

JUDEO-CHRISTIAN RELATIONS

Baeck, Leo. *Judaism and Christianity*. Philadelphia:
Jewish Publication Society of America, 1958.

Borowitz, Eugene B. *Contemporary Christologies: A Jewish Response.* Mahwah, N.J.: Paulist Press, 1980.

Bruce, F.F. *Israel and the Nations from the Exodus to the Fall of the Second Temple.* Grand Rapids, Mich.: Eerdmans, 1963. An interesting account by a Bible scholar.

Danielou, Jean. *The Theology of Jewish Christianity: The Development of Christian Doctrine Before the Council of Nicaea* (Vol. 1). John A. Baker, trans. London: Darten Longman and Todd; Chicago: Henry Regnery, 1964.

Davies, William David. *Christian Origin and Judaism.* Philadelphia: Westminster Press, 1962. A serious and scholarly examination of this timely subject.

Duvernoy, Claude. *Controversy of Zion.* Green Forest, Ark.: New Leaf Press, 1987.

Eckstein, Rabbi Yechiel. *What Christians Should Know About Jews and Judaism.* Waco, Tex.: Word Publishing, 1984.

Ellis, E. Earle. *Paul's Use of the Old Testament.* Grand Rapids, Mich.: Baker Book House, 1981.

Flannery, Edward H. *The Anguish of the Jews: Twenty-Six Centuries of Anti-Semitism* (rev. ed.). Mahwah, N.J.: Paulist Press, 1985.

Goldberg, Louis. *Our Jewish Friends* (rev. ed.). Neptune, N.J.: Loizeaux Brothers, 1983.

Hagner, Donald. *The Jewish Reclamation of Jesus.* Grand Rapids, Mich.: Zondervan/Academic Books, 1984.

Isaac, Jules. *The Teaching of Contempt: Christian Roots of Anti-Semitism.* New York: Holt, Rinehart and Winston, 1964.

Katz, Jacob. *Exclusiveness and Tolerance.* New York: Oxford Univ. Press, 1961. A unique discussion of Jewish-Christian relations in Medieval and modern times.

Lachs, Samuel Tobias. *A Rabbinic Commentary on the New Testament.* Hoboken, N.J.: Ktav Publishing House, 1987.

Lapide, Pinchas E. *Hebrew in the Church: The Foundations of Jewish-Christian Dialogue.* Grand Rapids, Mich.: Eerdmans, 1984.

———. *The Resurrection of Jesus: A Jewish Perspective.* Minneapolis, Minn.: Augsburg Publishing House, 1983.

Lapide, Pinchas E., and Ulrich Luz. *Jesus in Two Perspectives: A Jewish-Christian Dialogue.* Minneapolis, Minn.: Augsburg Publishing House, 1984.

Lapide, Pinchas E., and Jurgen Moltmann. *Jewish Monotheism and Christian Trinitarian Doctrine: A Dialogue by Pinchas Lapide and Jurgen Moltmann.* Philadelphia: Fortress Press, 1979.

Lapide, Pinchas E., and Peter Stuhlmacher. *Paul Rabbi and Apostle.* Minneapolis, Minn.: Augsburg Publishing House, 1984.

Limburg, James. *Judaism: An Introduction for Christians.* Minneapolis, Minn.: Augsburg Publishing House, 1987.

Moshe, Beth. *Judaism's Truth Answers the Missionaries.* New York: Bloch Publishing, 1987.

Newman, Louis I. *The Jewish People, Faith and Life: A Guide Book and Manual of Information Concerning Jewry and Judaism.* New York: Bloch Publishing, 1964.

Parkes, James William. *Judaism and Christianity.* Chicago: Univ. of Chicago Press, 1948.

———. *The Conflict of the Church and the Synagogue.* New York: New American Library/Meridian Books, 1961.

Pragai, Michael J. *Faith and Fulfillment: Christians and the Return to the Promised Land.* London: Valentine Mitchell, 1985.

Pruter, Carl. *Jewish Christians in the United States: A Bibliography.* New York: Garland Publishing, 1987.

Rudin, A. James. *Israel for Christians: Understanding Modern Israel.* Philadelphia: Fortress Press, 1983.

Rudin, A. James, and Marvin R. Wilson. *A Time to Speak.* Grand Rapids, Mich.: Baker Book House, 1987.

Runes, Dagobert B. *The Jew and the Cross.* New York: Philosophical Library, 1965.

Shermis, Michael. *Jewish Christian Relations: An Annotated Bibliography and Resource Guide.* Bloomington: Indiana Univ. Press, 1988.

Siegel, Gerald. *The Jew and the Christian Missionary: A Jewish Response to Missionary Christianity.* New York: Cataw Publishing House, 1981.

Stern, David H. *Messianic Jewish Manifesto.* Jerusalem: Jewish New Testament Publications, 1988.

Tannenbaum, Marc H., Marvin R. Wilson, and A. James Rudin, eds. *Evangelicals and Jews in an Age of Pluralism.* Grand Rapids, Mich.: Baker Book House, 1984.

———. *Evangelicals and Jews in Conversation.* Grand Rapids, Mich.: Baker Book House, 1978.

Wilson, Marvin R. *Our Father Abraham: Jewish Roots of the Christian Faith.* Grand Rapids, Mich.: Eerdmans, 1989.

WORKS BY JEWISH BELIEVERS

Edersheim, Alfred. *Sketches of Jewish Social Life in the Days of Christ.* Religious Tract Society, 1908. An authoritative study calculated to enlighten the serious Bible student.

————. *The Life and Times of Jesus the Messiah.* Grand Rapids, Mich.: Eerdmans, 1972. A definitive work.

Feinberg, Charles. *Israel at the Center of History and Revelation.* Portland, Ore.: Multnomah Press, 1980.

————. *Israel in the Light of Prophecy.* Chicago: Moody Press, 1964. A modern Hebrew-Christian scholar examines Israel's destiny from a prophetic perspective.

Fruchtenbaum, Arnold. *Hebrew Christianity: Its Theology, History, and Philosophy.* Grand Rapids, Mich.: Baker Book House, 1974.

Fuchs, Daniel. *Israel's Holy Days.* Neptune, N.J.: Loizeaux Brothers, 1987.

Gartenhaus, Jacob. *Christ Killers, Past and Present.* Chattanooga, Tenn.: Hebrew Christian Press, 1975.

————. *Famous Hebrew Christians.* Chattanooga, Tenn.: International Board of Jewish Missions, 1979.

Jocz, Jacob. *The Jewish People and Jesus Christ.* Grand Rapids, Mich.: Baker Book House, 1979. A leading theologian examines the problem of the Jewish people with the person and theological implications of Jesus and His ministry, and so forth.

————-. *The Spiritual History of Israel*. London: Eyre and Spotiswode, 1961.

Kac, Arthur. *The Death and Resurrection of Israel*. Grand Rapids, Mich.: Baker Book House, 1969. Sequel to *The Rebirth of the State of Israel*. Highly recommended.

————. *The Messianic Hope*. Grand Rapids, Mich.: Baker Book House, 1975.

————. *The Rebirth of the State of Israel*. Grand Rapids, Mich.: Baker Book House, 1958. An excellent study of the Biblical background and Scriptural implications of the reestablishment of the State of Israel.

Koser, Hilda. *Come and Get It!* Orlando, Fla.: Golden Rule Book Press, 1987.

Reich, Max I. *The Messianic Hope of Israel*. Chicago: Moody Press, 1945.

Rubin, Barry. *You Bring the Bagels, I'll Bring the Gospel*. Old Tappan, N.J.: Fleming H. Revell, 1989.

Schonfield, Hugh Joseph*. *History of Jewish Christianity from the First to the Twentieth Century*. London: Gerald Duckworth, 1936.

Urbach, Eliezer. *Out of the Fury*. Denver, Colo.: Zhera Publications, 1987.

MESSIAH IN JEWISH THOUGHT

Driver, S.R., and A.D. Neubauer. *The Fifty-Third Chapter of Isaiah According to the Jewish Interpreters.*

---

*At the time H.J. Schonfield wrote this text, he claimed to be a believer in Jesus as the Messiah. This is no longer true.

Hoboken, N.J.: Ktav Publishing House, 1877.

Fredricks, Ernest, William S. Green, and Jacob Neusner. *Judaisms and Their Messiahs at the Turn of the Christian Era.* New York: Cambridge Univ. Press, 1987.

Greenstone, Julius H. *The Messiah Idea in Jewish History.* Jewish Publication Society of America, 1906.

Klausner, Joseph. *The Messianic Idea in Israel.* New York: Macmillan, 1955.

Patai, Raphael. *The Messiah Texts: Jewish Legends of Three Thousand Years.* Detroit: Wayne State Univ. Press, 1979.

Scholem, Gershom. *The Messianic Idea in Judaism and Other Essays on Jewish Spirituality.* New York: Schocken Books, 1987.

Serachek, Joseph. *The Doctrine of Messiah in Medieval Jewish Literature.* New York: Harmon Press, 1968.

Silver, Abba-Hillel. *A History of Messianic Speculation in Israel.* Gloucester, Mass.: Peter Smith, 1987.

CHOSEN PEOPLE MINISTRIES' PRODUCTS

Bell, John. *How to Be Like the Messiah: Walking the New Halakhah.* Charlotte, N.C.: Chosen People Ministries, 1987. A discipleship guide for Jewish believers.

Fuchs, Daniel, and Harold A. Sevener. *From Bondage to Freedom.* Neptune, N.J.: Loizeaux Brothers, 1995. Deals with the "400 silent years" between the close of the Old Testament and the opening of the New.

Sevener, Harold A. *Daniel: God's Man in Babylon.* Baltimore, Md., Lederer Messianic Ministries, 1995. A comprehensive study of the Book of Daniel.

1 800- 423 8743 -AKZO Noble

AKZO Noble/chemical division

Eagle High Reach

For a free copy of a catalog of books, tapes,
and videos available through
CHOSEN PEOPLE MINISTRIES,
call 1-800-333-4936.